JeSUS=fRiendS

what messages do you send to your friends?

Do you send many emails? How many txt msgs do you send each day?

What would you think if you got this text?

Jesus wnts 2 B ur frend

Who might it be from?

But what does that message mean?

What would you do about it?

Who is Jesus?

Jesus is God's Son.

God the Father sent him to be born as a baby over 2,000 years ago. He grew up and lived as a human being, just like all of us. But at the same time, Jesus was God – God as a human being! God did this to show everyone how much he loves us and to show us the sort of people he wants us to be.

Jesus made sick people better. He was friends with people no one else liked. He told great stories. He cared for younger people.

why does Jesus want you to be his friend?

What do you do with your friends?

Have a laugh together.

Talk together.

Chill together.

When Jesus lived on earth anyone could talk with him about anything! They could laugh together, do things together. Jesus wants to be a friend like that.

But if Jesus lived 2,000 years ago, how can anyone be his friend?

Some people didn't like what Jesus said – he said people might appear to do lots of good things, but inside they were not as good as they looked. They didn't like it when Jesus said he was God.

Some people didn't like what Jesus did – he was friends with no-hopers, those no one else liked, taxmen who were cheats, people struggling with disabilities.

None of us can love God as much as we should or be the person God wants us to be. Everyone who has ever lived (except Jesus) has been a cheat, told lies, been selfish, even though sometimes no one knows except us. Someone has to take the blame for that and be punished. That's only fair!

Some people hated Jesus so much that, even though he had never done anything wrong, they had him nailed to a cross and he died! He was being punished for all the wrong things all people have ever done.

The Bible says: "But God shows his great love for us in this way. Christ died for us while we were still sinners."

Romans 5:8

if Jesus died, how can you be his friend now?

Yes, he did die. But that's not the end of the story.

Three days later he came alive again.

His friends talked with him.

They even had a barbecue together.

They knew Jesus really was alive.

Then Jesus went back to God his Father in heaven. In his place he sent his Holy Spirit.

Just like we can't see the wind, we cannot see the Holy Spirit but we know he is there.

The Holy Spirit is 'God everywhere'.

This means that Jesus, who is God, can be with us too, all the time, whatever we are doing.

So what's the point of being Jesus' friend?

When Jesus came alive again, he had a new body, a new life.

He had been punished for all the wrong things we have done but now wants to forgive us and give us a fresh new start.

Jesus was human like us. He knows what it is like to be tempted to do things we know are wrong.

The Holy Spirit can help us say "No!" when we are tempted.

And even if we do go wrong again, God will still forgive us if we are sorry and really mean it.

Jesus can be with us as a friend wherever we are. A friend of Jesus is never really alone.

The more time we spend with our friends, the more we become like them.

The Holy Spirit slowly changes us so that we begin to think, speak and behave like Jesus.

Like Jesus, we begin to care more for other people.

> **The Bible says, "The Spirit produces the fruit of love, joy, peace, patience, kindness, goodness, faithfulness, gentleness, self-control."**
>
> **Galatians 5:22–23**

So how can you become a friend of Jesus?

Thank God that he loves you.

Say sorry for all the wrong things you have done.

Ask Jesus to forgive you and become your friend.

Remember that the Holy Spirit will be with you wherever you are.

> **The Bible says, "God loved the world so much that he gave his one and only Son so that whoever believes in him may not be lost, but have eternal life."**
>
> **John 3:16**

You need to talk with Jesus. Use these words or make up your own. He'll hear you, whatever you say!

Jesus, I want to be your friend. Thank you that you love me. Thank you for living in the world and dying on a cross for me. I'm sorry for all the wrong things I've done. Please forgive me and let me be your friend. Please let the Holy Spirit help me be like you. Amen.	Write your own words here...

So now what do you do?

Tune in to Jesus by reading or listening to the Bible, or talking with other people who are Jesus' friends.

Talk with Jesus about what you are happy or sad about.

Expect God to help you live in a way that pleases him.

Psst: You don't need to use any special words or close your eyes or go to a special place. You can talk out loud to God or you can keep what you want to say in your head.

Do things which please God, with the help of the Holy Spirit.

For example...

Tell the truth and watch what you say.

Help people in need.

Try to include those who no one else likes.

Hang out with other friends of Jesus so that you can...

Talk with him together.

Remind yourself you're not the only friend of Jesus.

Help each other be more like Jesus.

Ask the person who gave you **Jesus=friendship forever** to tell you about a club for friends of Jesus, in your school, in a church or somewhere else in your community. It may not be possible for you to meet with others. If so, ask this person to give you a Bible and a guide booklet to help you. And ask them to pray for you often!

There are millions of friends of Jesus. You can be one of them too!